THE TRICKSTER SHOWDOWN

LOKI

VS

HERMES

by Claudia Oviedo

CAPSTONE PRESS
a capstone imprint

Published by Capstone Press, an imprint of Capstone
1710 Roe Crest Drive, North Mankato, Minnesota 56003
capstonepub.com

Library of Congress Cataloging-in-Publication Data is available
on the Library of Congress website.
ISBN: 9781666343762 (hardcover)
ISBN: 9781666343779 (paperback)
ISBN: 9781666343786 (ebook PDF)

Summary: It's a battle of the clever troublemaker versus the great thief.
The Norse god Loki loves creating chaos wherever he goes, showing
his power by stirring up trouble for the gods. The cunning Greek god
Hermes serves as a messenger to the gods and Zeus's personal thief. If
these two gods were to go head-to-head, who would come out on top?

Editorial Credits
Editor: Julie Gassman; Designer: Heidi Thompson; Media Researcher:
Jo Miller; Production Specialist: Tori Abraham

Image Credits
Alamy: Album, 9, ART Collection, 27 (Left), Artokoloro, 29,
ATStockFoto, 26, BFA, 25, Ivy Close Images, 17, Lebrecht Music &
Arts, 19, Michelle Bridges, 7, 15, Science History Images, 27 (Right);
Getty Images: Picturenow, 23, Print Collector, 13; Shutterstock: Atelier
Sommerland, Cover (Bottom), 5, creativica, Cover (Top), Evgeny
Komzolov, 11, iobard, 21, Liliya Butenko, 10, Maltiase, 12, Mari
Dandelion, 4, 28, Racheal Grazias, 18, Superstock/Pantheon, 20

All internet sites appearing in back matter were available and accurate
when this book was sent to press.

TABLE OF CONTENTS

Words in **bold** are in the glossary.

THE TRICKSTERS

In mythology, some gods were known as **tricksters**. Tricksters were clever. They liked playing pranks. They were troublemakers. But they were not always bad, nor did they always mean harm. Loki, the **Norse** god of mischief, is one example. Hermes, the Greek god of thieves, is another.

Loki

FACT

A mythology is a set of stories called **myths** that explain things about the world around us. In myths, tricksters often have the job of testing the rules.

What would happen if Loki and Hermes met in battle? Who would be the most clever? What kind of trouble would they make for each other? Who would win the title of biggest trickster?

Hermes

THE TRICKSTERS' BEGINNINGS

Loki was the Norse god of mischief. There are no popular myths about his birth or youth. The myths describe him as half god. His mother was the leaf goddess Laufey. His father was the giant Fárbauti. The giants, called the Jotun, were the powerful beings in Norse mythology that existed before the gods.

Neither of Loki's parents was particularly powerful. Loki decided to surround himself with other strong gods. He swore brotherhood to Odin, chief of the Norse gods. This made him an uncle of sorts to Odin's famous son, Thor. Loki later joined Thor in many adventures.

Loki (left) often helped Thor (right) by coming up with clever plans.

Hermes was the Greek god of thieves and travel. He had many powerful relatives. He was very close with his father, Zeus, king of the gods. His mother was Maia, a daughter of the **Titan** Atlas. Titans were the powerful beings that existed before the gods.

Hermes was clever even as a baby, though he did not receive his best-known powers until later. As a newborn, he stole 50 cows from his older brother Apollo, just for the fun of it. He hid the cows in a cave. He covered his tracks by tying brooms to the cows' tails. Apollo was furious. Hermes swore he had nothing to do with it. But Zeus could see through him.

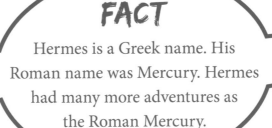

FACT

Hermes is a Greek name. His Roman name was Mercury. Hermes had many more adventures as the Roman Mercury.

Hermes's brother Apollo was the Greek god of music, poetry, and art.

BAGS OF TRICKS

Loki had the power to **shape-shift**, but his greatest skill was his wit. In one myth, Loki stole the hair of Thor's wife as a joke. Thor was angry. Loki promised to replace the hair.

Thor was known as the god of thunder.

Loki asked some dwarfs to make new hair, along with a few magical items. They agreed, in exchange for his head. Loki shape-shifted into a fly to distract them from finishing and claiming their payment.

But the dwarfs did finish. They pulled out their knives to collect their payment. Loki said he promised them his head, not his neck. Since they couldn't take one without the other, Loki was saved.

Gungnir and Mjolnir

Odin's spear and Thor's hammer were among the magical items Loki tricked the dwarfs into making. The spear, called Gungnir, always hit its mark. The hammer, known as Mjolnir, always returned to its thrower. Loki had no magical weapons of his own.

Hermes's honesty led to his greatest power. It was the ability to go anywhere. When he was a baby, Hermes invented a musical instrument called the lyre. He gave it to Apollo, who was the god of music, as an apology for stealing his cows. He promised not to lie again.

lyre

As a reward for telling the truth about the cows, Zeus made Hermes messenger of the gods. He could go anywhere he wanted to. He could even travel to the **underworld**! In this role, Hermes served many gods and helped many heroes in their quests.

Gifts for Hermes

Zeus gave Hermes winged sandals called the talaria. These sandals helped him fly fast. Apollo gave Hermes the caduceus. This staff had two **serpents** twisted around it. It helped Hermes to travel anywhere freely.

Hermes's special skill was speed, thanks to his sandals, the talaria.

GODS GONE BAD

Loki's tricks were sometimes harmful. He was occasionally a **villain**. One myth involved Thor's brother, Balder, the god of light. Balder could not be harmed. The rest of the gods played a game of throwing things at Balder just to watch them bounce off of him. Loki grew bored of the game. He shape-shifted into an old lady. Then, he tricked Balder's mother into telling him Balder's weakness, mistletoe.

Next, Loki tricked Balder's blind twin brother into throwing a stick of mistletoe at Balder. The mistletoe killed Balder instantly. The gods tried to bring him back from the underworld, but they failed. They didn't think twice about punishing Loki this time. They locked him up in a cave under the earth with a serpent above him dripping **venom** on his head.

Disguised as an old woman, Loki tricked Balder's
mother into trusting him.

Hermes was rarely the villain like Loki was, but he was seldom the hero of the story. He was usually a helper. His power to go anywhere made him very useful to other gods.

In one myth, Hermes helped the hero Perseus. He got him the tools he needed to defeat the monster Medusa. He also led Perseus to her. In another myth, Hermes helped Hercules complete the last of his famous 12 **labors**. He led the hero into the underworld to find Cerberus, the three-headed dog.

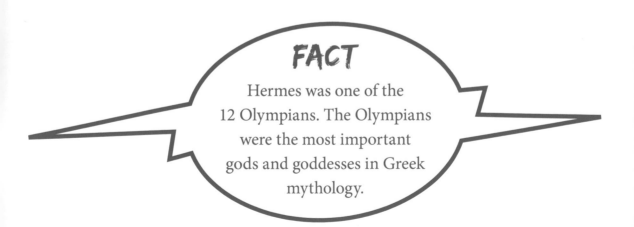

FACT

Hermes was one of the 12 Olympians. The Olympians were the most important gods and goddesses in Greek mythology.

Perseus (left) and Hermes (right) were half brothers. Zeus was their father.

Hermes never outgrew his stealing habit. But even by stealing, he sometimes helped others. For example, Hermes stole his little brother Ares from giants. Ares, the god of war, had been locked away in a jar for more than a year. Hermes kept stealing, sometimes at the request of Zeus. He stole the belt of Aphrodite and Poseidon's **trident**.

Poseidon used his trident to form thunderstorms and tidal waves.

TAKING ON DEATH

The Norse gods are not **immortal.** They will die one day. The myth called Ragnarök tells about the future death of many gods, including Loki. In the myth, Balder's death will start a war among gods and giants. Loki will escape his punishment for his part in Balder's death. Then he will get **revenge** on the gods for punishing him.

During Ragnarök, giants and monsters will attack the gods.

Loki will lead an army of giants, including his children, against the gods. There is Hel and her army of dead soldiers from the underworld. There is the serpent Jörmungandr, who will flood the seas and kill Thor with his poison. Finally, there is the wolf Fenrir, who will eat the sun and kill Odin.

The gods captured Fenrir using a magic chain, but the wolf will break free at Ragnarök.

Heimdall will sound a horn to warn the gods the giants are coming at the start of Ragnarök.

Loki, himself, will fight the god Heimdall. They will kill each other. Meanwhile, Loki's army will set the world on fire, killing humans, giants, and gods. The world will then sink into the sea. Lucky for us, the world will rise again and start over.

The Greek gods are immortal, and Hermes will never die. Yet Hermes formed a special relationship with death. He was the one who brought the souls of the dead to the River Styx. This river led the way to the underworld, where souls went after death. Hermes could go there and return to Earth freely. This was thanks to his power of travel.

Hermes used his knowledge to help others. In one myth, he brought Persephone back to Earth with him. Persephone was the queen of the underworld. She had been tricked into becoming queen. Hermes helped her stay on Earth long enough to see her mother. This brought her peace.

Persephone (right) greeted her mother (left) with Hermes by her side.

THEY LIVE ON

People continue to read and write about both trickster gods. Thor and Odin were the biggest heroes of Norse mythology. However, Loki appears in almost as many myths as those two gods. Today, Loki is even more popular than Odin. He appears in various video games and books, including the Magnus Chase books by Rick Riordan.

Loki also appears in Marvel comics and movies. He is at Thor's side in many of these. Loki has even gone from bad guy to good guy. In 2021, he got his own TV series. In it, Loki is trying to save the world. He has hero status once more.

FACT

Loki is not Thor's uncle in the Marvel Universe. They are brothers. Traditionally, Loki has red hair, but Marvel made his hair black.

An advertisement for the Disney+ TV series, *Loki*, starring Tom Hiddleston

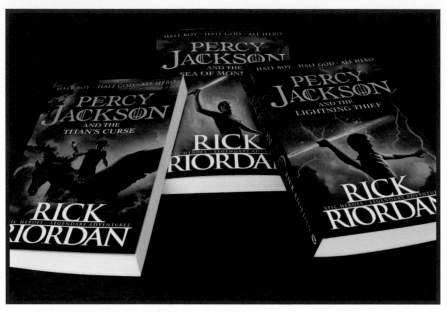

Hermes is a helper to Percy Jackson in the books and movies.

Meanwhile, Hermes appears in more myths than any other Greek god, as well as many ancient poems and plays. But he is rarely the hero in these ancient works.

Even in new stories, Hermes does not get his turn at being the hero. He is a supporting character in various video games and in Disney's animated movie *Hercules*. In the Percy Jackson books and movies by Rick Riordan, Hermes gives Percy tools and advice, just as he did to the ancient heroes.

Loki and Hermes came from different cultures. Yet they are very similar in some ways. How would you imagine a battle between the two? Who has the power to win? Who has the smarts? Who is the best trickster?

Loki

Hermes

LOKI VS. HERMES AT A GLANCE

Name:	Loki
God of:	Mischief and fire
Appearance:	Handsome, thin, and red-haired
Weapons:	None
Strengths:	Wit
Powers and abilities:	Shape-shifter
Weaknesses:	Harms others
Symbol:	None, but sometimes thought to be snakes

Name:	Hermes
God of:	Messenger of the gods and god of thieves and travelers
Appearance:	Handsome and athletic, beardless when young, often bearded when older
Weapons:	His staff, the caduceus, and his flying sandals, the talaria, were considered weapons by some
Strengths:	Clever
Powers and abilities:	Speed and ability to travel anywhere
Weaknesses:	Could not stop stealing
Symbol:	Caduceus (two serpents wrapped around a staff)

GLOSSARY

immortal (i-MOR-tuhl)—living forever and never dying

labors (LAY-bors)—12 nearly impossible feats that Hercules had to complete as a punishment

myth (MITH)—a story from ancient times; myths often tried to explain natural events

Norse (NORS)—related to ancient Scandinavia

revenge (ri-VENJ)—to hurt as a form of getting back at

serpent (SER-puhnt)—a large, snakelike creature

shape-shift (SHAYP-shift)—the ability to transform oneself into another person, animal, or creature

Titan (TIE-tuhn)—a member of the ancient and original family of gods before the Olympians

trickster (TRIK-ster)—a character who plays tricks or causes trouble in myths

trident (TRY-dent)—a spear with three sharp points at its end

underworld (UHN-dur-wurld)—the mythical land of the dead

venom (VEN-uhm)—a poison produced by some animals

villain (VIL-uhn)—a character who does harmful things in a story

READ MORE

Aperlo, Peter. *Introduction to Norse Mythology for Kids: A Fun Collection of the Greatest Heroes, Monsters, and Gods in Norse Myth*. Berkeley, CA: Ulysses Press, 2021.

Marcus, Richard, Natalie Buczynsky, and Jonathan Shelnutt. *Introduction to Greek Mythology for Kids: A Fun Collection of the Best Heroes, Monsters, and Gods in Greek Myth*. Berkeley, CA: Ulysses Press, 2021.

Ralphs, Matt. *Norse Myths: Meet the Gods, Monsters, and Heroes of the Vikings*. New York: DK Publishing, 2021.

INTERNET SITES

The Gods and Goddesses of Ancient Greece!
natgeokids.com/uk/discover/history/greece/greek-gods/

Greek Mythology: Hermes
ducksters.com/history/ancient_greece/hermes.php

Viking Primary Resource: Old Norse Gods
natgeokids.com/uk/primary-resource/viking-primary-resource-old-norse-gods/

INDEX

ABOUT THE AUTHOR

Claudia Oviedo writes for children under various names. Reading about different mythologies with her kids is a favorite pastime. Claudia has received several honors for her work. They include 2009 Paterson Prize for Books for Young People, as well as the 2008 and 2015 Texas Institute of Letters Best Young Adult Book Award, and several starred reviews for her picture books.